Take the Leap: Starting Your Own Company

Marlize Maree

Chapter 1: Introduction to Starting Your Own Company

Understanding the Entrepreneurial Mindset

Becoming an entrepreneur is a complex undertaking that involves more than just coming up with a winning concept and a strong business plan. It requires an entrepreneurial mindset, which is a concoction of traits and characteristics essential for negotiating the turbulent seas of entrepreneurship. This chapter explores the essential elements of this mindset, including drive, passion, creativity, risk-taking, resilience, and inventiveness, and explains how to develop each to support your entrepreneurial efforts.

Reflecting on my own journey from corporate executive boardrooms to leading my marketing agency, I can attest to the practical use of these theoretical concepts. Nearly four years into this, the road is still difficult and full of obstacles that put my will to the test every day. Yet, it's within this never-ending grind that I've discovered true satisfaction.

Taking risks was the first thing that got me out of corporate security and into the chaos of being an entrepreneur. This jump showed me how to embrace the unknown, which is something I had studied before but only fully understood after putting my job at risk.

Even the word "resilience" changed what it meant when it wasn't in a business book. Every problem with my business has been a personal test, from money problems to problems with clients. Reading about getting back up is one thing, but going down and getting back up is quite another.

Innovation and creativity have consistently been with me, which has helped me respond quickly to changes in the market. Big companies are like "big passenger ships." My agency, on the other hand, is like a "speed boat"—nimble and quick to change. This flexibility has been a key differentiator, which is similar to what an entrepreneurial mindset is supposed to do.

There have been times when getting out of bed seemed like an impossible task, but the fact that I am passionate about this hobby of mine has prevented me from becoming exhausted. Meeting with customers who bring about positive changes in my life and observing how the market evolves are the things that keep me motivated.

This serves as an illustration of how important it is to have a deep love for the business that you run.

Individual experiences like these lend credibility to the concepts that support developing an entrepreneurial mindset. The fact that they bring abstract ideas to life demonstrates that becoming an entrepreneur is about more than just adopting a certain set of attitudes. This is about putting those attitudes into action in the world that we actually live in.

Let's break down these essential components of an entrepreneurial mindset as you progress through this chapter. We will do this by drawing on both theoretical concepts and the practical experiences of someone who is already in the business of being an entrepreneur. I hope that by combining these different points of view, I will be able to provide you with an in-depth understanding of what it takes to be successful in the challenging yet exciting world of business ownership.

Researching market opportunities

I remember clearly the day I realised what was missing in the Namibian marketing world. I couldn't believe I was able to identify the problem and provide a solution. The clarity with which I saw this opportunity, as well as my ability to envision how to make it a reality, were both exciting. Everything I'd been through seemed to have come together to give me the knowledge and confidence I needed to take advantage of this opportunity.

It is necessary to have a great deal of knowledge about the market in order to launch a successful business. Investigating the possibilities presented by the market is not merely a step; rather, it is a vital part of being an entrepreneur. This process involves taking an in-depth look at trends, consumer behaviour, and the competition in order to make the right strategic decisions.

The first important step is to figure out who your target market is. To make a relevant and compelling value proposition, you need to know who your customers are, what they want, and what they value. Finding a gap in the market in Namibia that wasn't being met was the first step on my journey.

On top of that, it is important to take a look at the competition. It indicates where there are gaps in the market and where you have the opportunity to differentiate yourself. My understanding of the market and the businesses in it made my search for a distinctive gap for my agency simpler.

It is essential to stay abreast of the ever-evolving needs of your customers and the trends that are occurring in your industry. This guarantees your capacity to remain relevant and adaptable in the face of shifting market conditions. As a result of my dedication to staying informed, I have been able to adjust to the changing market conditions and perform well.

To start market research, you need to have a clear idea of who your target audience is. Figure out who your possible customers are by listing their age, gender, income, and buying habits. First, look at the data you already have, do some surveys, or talk to potential customers in person or through focus groups or interviews. Next, you should look at your competitors. List your main rivals, evaluate what they offer, their pros and cons, and figure out what makes your business unique. Read as much as you can about what is happening in the world; make sure you know what is going on; and lastly, talk to your customers; make sure you spend quality time with them. This all-around approach will not only help you understand your position in the market, but it will also show you how to be innovative and stand out, giving your business strategy a solid base.

Finding a unique niche in Namibian marketing was a turning point for me. It was the point where all of my experiences and knowledge came together. Realising what the market was missing made me better at finding and filling gaps, and it also made me realise how important it is to know the market well in order to run a successful business. I hope this will help you understand the importance of research and knowing who you are talking to. Do not skip this step.

Chapter 2: Developing Your Business Idea

Brainstorming potential business ideas

Coming up with business ideas isn't just a fun activity; it's also an important step towards becoming an entrepreneur. It requires matching your interests and skills with what the market wants and where it wants to go in the future. Finding out what you love and what you're good at will help you build a business idea that you'll be passionate about and that is more likely to succeed.

Always keep in mind the problems or needs that your business could solve in the market. By combining this data with your understanding of current and future trends, you can come up with a concept that will be relevant now and in the future.

Still, coming up with a concept is merely the beginning. If you put in the time and effort to study the market and get feedback from actual people, you can make sure that your business is fulfilling a need while also pursuing your passion. Basically, it's about laying the groundwork for a company's success through intelligent, informed decision-making.

As I became an entrepreneur, my experience in the fast-moving consumer goods (FMCG) industry and my deep love for advertising and branding helped me a lot. It's always interested me to figure out how a customer comes to a purchase and what drives them. It was this one-of-a-kind mix of branding and trade marketing that became the foundation of my marketing agency. Seeing a clear need in the market and combining my interests was not only exciting; it was also the spark that started my business idea.

By doing some brainstorming, I was able to find the one-of-a-kind spot where my interests and the requirements of the market met. I encourage people who are interested in becoming entrepreneurs to gain a deeper understanding of their areas of expertise and areas of interest. Your idea for a business should not only excite you, but it should also satisfy a clearly identified need or gap in the market.

As important as the initial brainstorming session is the process of conducting market research and gaining a comprehensive understanding of your competitive landscape. We touched on this in the previous chapter, but by repeating it, I just want to highlight how important market research is. Remember, knowledge is power.

My personal experience in the fast-moving consumer goods industry taught me the importance of having a comprehensive understanding of your market. Because of this understanding, you will be able to precisely tailor your offerings and differentiate yourself in a market that is already quite competitive.

Last but not least, make sure you put your business idea through its paces. Prove that your concept has a leg up in the real world and can permanently meet the needs of your intended audience.

These steps can help you ensure your business idea is solid:

Conduct Market Research: Start by researching your target market to understand their needs, preferences, and pain points. Look for gaps in the market that your business idea can fill, and identify potential competitors.

Test Your Idea: Consider creating a minimum viable product (MVP) or prototype to test your business idea with a small group of potential customers. Gather feedback and make any necessary adjustments to improve your product or service.

Seek Feedback: Don't be afraid to reach out to friends, family, mentors, or industry experts for feedback on your business idea. Their insights can help you refine your concept and identify potential challenges.

Analyse Data: Use data analytics tools to track and analyse customer behaviour, market trends, and other relevant metrics. This data can provide valuable insights into the viability of your business idea.

Create a Business Plan: Develop a comprehensive business plan that outlines your business goals, target market, competitive analysis, marketing strategies, and financial projections. A well-thought-out business plan will help you attract investors and secure funding for your business.

Going into business for yourself is both an art and a science. It all starts with a spark of passion, but to really succeed, you need to put in a lot of work and really understand the market. My own path shows this mix of creativity and strategic thinking. It shows that with the right approach, your business idea can grow from an idea to a business that is ready to go to market.

Chapter 3: Creating a Business Plan

Writing an Executive Summary

Your executive summary is the first thing people will see when they look at your business plan. It should grab the attention of potential investors or partners right away. It briefly explains your business idea, its unique qualities, your goals, and your strategies. It sets the tone for the more in-depth explanations that will come later in your business plan.

When writing an executive summary, you need to be clear, brief, and powerful. Start by giving a clear and convincing summary of your business idea, focusing on what makes it special and how it can be sold. Write down your short- and long-term business goals and make sure they fit with the overall direction of your company. A complete picture of your business can be gained by looking at your target market, your competitors, your marketing efforts, and your strategic partnerships. The summary should end with a strong conclusion that emphasises how appealing your business is as an investment. This part should be carefully polished to get rid of any uncertainty or faults.

My experience has taught me that writing the executive summary last in a business plan delivers the best results. Your vision and strategy can be shaped by reading the business plan in its entirety; then, you could use this information to craft an effective executive summary. In this approach, the summary is guaranteed to serve as more than merely an introduction. It demonstrates that you have given your business plan a lot of thought and that it accurately reflects your company's values and goals. Going through the process of detailed planning will help you write a more effective and persuasive summary. By using this method, an in-depth knowledge of your business and useful insights are bound to be clear after reviewing, and you can easily summarise your company plan's key points into a clear overview while maintaining the clarity and coherence that come from a thorough understanding of the entire document.

Defining Your Target Market

Knowing who you're selling to and how to reach them is crucial to the success of your business. You shouldn't just think about the people you think will buy your goods and services; you should also think about the people who really need or want them. In order to better serve your potential customers, it is a good idea to perform thorough market research to learn about their demographic and psychographic characteristics.

Knowing your target market is more than just knowing their age, gender, and income. By looking into psychographics, like interests, values, and lifestyles, you can learn more about what drives your customers and make your products and services more in line with what they want and expect. You can be sure that your products or services will help them by finding out what they want, need, and are having trouble with.

Additionally, it is of the utmost importance to determine the size of your target market as well as the economic potential it possesses. What it tells you is whether or not there is a significant demand for what you are selling, which is essential for the continued success and expansion of your company over the long term.

Working for SABMiller in Namibia taught me how important it is to really get to know the people you want to reach. I saw for myself how our MD's strong drive for face-to-face interactions with consumers in their own environment had a big effect on how we did marketing. Carling Black Label was just one of many things that we discussed; the most important thing it did was give us the chance to listen and see what our people wanted from us and CBL as a brand. Carling Black Label became the second-largest beer brand in Namibia, largely because of this grassroots strategy. Nothing beats spending time with your customer in their environment, experiencing their pain points firsthand.

A connection can be made between the experience at SABMiller and the theories that are involved in determining who your target market is. In order to effectively define a market, it is essential to have a deeper understanding of the market than just the surface level, as we discovered through our actual interactions in Namibia. This involves getting intimately familiar with the market, engaging in conversations with potential customers, and gathering information that would be impossible to obtain through conventional market research.

The theory stresses how important it is to do a lot of research and look at a lot of data in order to find a target market. In real life, as I saw, this data-driven approach, along with real, face-to-face customer engagement, gives you a fuller, more accurate picture of your target market. The combination of theory and practice gives any business a strong headstart to find and deeply understand its core audience.

Developing a marketing strategy

In order for a small business to be successful, it is essential to have a solid marketing plan. This plan will assist you in connecting with your ideal customers, highlighting the unique value that you offer, and increasing sales. First and foremost, you need to have a solid understanding of your target audience. It is essential to get a good understanding of their actions, wants, and needs in order to compose messages that will stick with them. Since we have already gone over this topic in great detail in the previous section, it is now time to put everything in writing.

The next critical stage is to identify your USP. This is the secret ingredient to your product's success in a competitive market. A compelling unique selling proposition (USP) is more than just a feature; it is the customer's response to the question "why you?" and it ought to be integrated into all of your marketing efforts.

To get your message out there, you need to know your USP and who you want to reach. Then you can plan the best mix of marketing strategies. Whether you're using digital campaigns, content marketing, or good ol' fashioned ads, it's important to have clear standards to ensure that every marketing strategy you employ helps you achieve your marketing goals.

Despite my extensive background in marketing, I found the process of developing a strategy for my own company to be surprisingly challenging. It went to show that even the most knowledgeable people can become paralysed by their own thoughts occasionally. My lesson here is that clarity and simplicity are key when communicating and planning. Once I zeroed in on the fundamentals—understanding my target demographic and the features that set my brand apart—things began to fall into place. This pulled me back to the basic truth: a good strategy is a plan that is clear, well-understood, and doable.

This journey of mine is similar to the steps you would take in a classroom to do a marketing plan, but it adds a practical element by showing you how important it is to be clear and focused. Planning can get complicated, but remembering to base your strategy on two basic ideas—understanding your audience and figuring out what makes your business unique—will help you keep your cool.

It takes both art and science to come up with a marketing plan. It takes both careful analysis and creative thinking, along with a deep knowledge of the market and a clear picture of how your brand fits into it. The process of planning for my own business taught me how important it is to keep things simple and on track. Target audience insight and a compelling unique selling proposition (USP) are two of the most important parts of making a marketing strategy. If you stick to these, you can make a strong plan that helps your business reach its goals.

Chapter 4: Legal and Financial Considerations

Choosing a Business Structure

An entrepreneur is faced with a number of important decisions, one of the most important of which is selecting the appropriate business structure. This decision has implications for things like your personal responsibility, taxes, and legal obligations, in addition to other aspects of running a business. In order to ensure that the legal structure of your company is in line with your operational and financial objectives, it is essential to have a thorough understanding of the distinctions that exist between the various types of business structures, such as a sole proprietorship, partnership, limited liability company, or corporation.

Depending on the type of business structure, there are a variety of effects that impact control, liability, taxation, and administrative requirements. As an illustration, a sole proprietorship is simple to manage and provides you with direct control; however, it does not shield you from personal liability in the same way that a limited liability company or a corporation does. On the other hand, corporations provide a higher level of liability protection and structured management, but they also require a higher level of compliance and more detailed reporting.

Once you've chosen the best structure for your business, the next important step is to register it. This official recognition from the law lets you legally do business, pay your taxes, and get the licences and permits you need. It includes picking a name for your business, registering it with state and local authorities, and following all the rules that are specific to your type of business and location.

Setting up my own business was a process that required me to think about things and plan ahead. Because of how partnerships work, picking a proprietary limited company (Pty) was a choice made on purpose to protect everyone legally and set clear expectations for accountability. We needed a more formal arrangement, and this structure met our needs. It required annual audits and made it clear who was responsible for what and how they were protected. It taught me how important it is to make sure that the structure of a business fits with the type of ownership, the operational goals, and the level of legal protection I want.

The time it took to think about the options, compare them, and make a decision made it clear how important this choice was for establishing the legal and operational identity of the business. It really is of the utmost importance to understand what each structure means and to make sure you know exactly what is needed in your own business.

Choosing the appropriate organisational structure for your company and ensuring that it is properly registered are both essential first steps on the path to becoming an ambitious business owner. In a practical and legal sense, they establish the guidelines that will govern the operation of your company. A partnership structure was the one I went with because of the way my partnership operates. This demonstrates how these theoretical points can be applied in real life, highlighting the fact that you need to take a different approach in order to make the decision that is most suitable for the unique needs of your company.

Managing Finances and Budgeting

For individuals who are interested in beginning their own businesses, having knowledge of finances is not merely a skill; it is a requirement. In order for a company to continue operating and expanding, it is necessary to have a budget and to have good financial management. Beginning this journey with a well-organised budget provides you with a clear picture of your income and expenses, which enables you to make intelligent decisions and maintain the stability of your finances.

The first step towards being financially responsible is to create a comprehensive budget for yourself. Similar to a map for your finances, this document reveals the source of your money as well as the ultimate destinations of your money. You are able to find ways to save money, make the most of the money you have, and improve your financial position as a result of this vision.

Not only is it essential to create a budget, but it is also of the utmost importance to maintain accurate financial records. Using this method, you will have a comprehensive record of all financial transactions, which will provide you with a solid foundation of information that you can use to evaluate the financial health of your company and plan for its future.

Going back to your financial plan on a regular basis and making adjustments to it as your company expands is another important thing to do. This constant cycle ensures that your financial strategy continues to align with the way in which your company is evolving, which in turn makes it more adaptable and resilient.

The ways in which I have personally dealt with managing my finances have been difficult but informative. Since I have a background in marketing, I have the skills necessary to make money, but I do not always have the skills necessary to manage it. Once I realised this, I came to the conclusion that I needed a financial manager on board. The decision to hire someone who could manage the finances but also had the balls to say "no" to me was a game-changer for my company. It made a very important point abundantly clear: it is very important to be aware of both your strengths and weaknesses, and there are times when the best thing to do is to delegate significant responsibilities to individuals who are more skilled in those areas.

For business owners who have had similar problems managing their money, the message is clear: hire a professional to handle your money. This investment not only protects the financial health of your business, but it also gives you the freedom to focus on what you do best, which will help you move your business forward with confidence and clarity.

Budgeting and managing money may not come naturally to all business owners, but they are necessary for the success of any business. The story of my journey adds to the theoretical tips in this chapter and shows that sometimes you need to rely on other people's knowledge to manage your money well. Accept that self-awareness and professional help can work together to help your business not only stay alive but also grow financially.

Chapter 5: Building Your Brand

Choosing a Memorable Business Name

Selecting a name that customers will easily remember is one of the most essential steps in the process of starting a new business. Not only is it a label, but it is also the first thing that people notice about your brand and the first thing that people interact with when they find it in the market.

A good name is like a beacon—it draws people in and shows what you stand for. Here are some important rules to follow as you come up with names:

It's important that your business name is clear and easy to remember. This simplicity makes it easier to find online and spreads the word about the business. Customers might not be able to connect with your brand if its name is hard to understand or complicated.

Think about the personality of your business. Is it fun or serious, new or old-fashioned? You should think of your brand's name as a mirror that shows the kind of experience people can expect.

While fads may come and go, it's important to focus on the long-term success of your company. Pick a name that will remain relevant even after a few years; stay away from cliches and other expressions that could seem archaic.

Despite its significance, people often overlook the step of ensuring your name is not already in use or trademarked. Simply conducting a quick search on the internet can assist you in avoiding potential legal issues in the future and ensuring that your name is unique.

Involving people you know, including friends, family, and potential customers, in the process of naming something can provide you with unexpected insights and ideas that can assist you in making a better choice that will appeal to your audience.

I recall talking to a lot of people about the company and my goals for it, especially friends who worked in the industry. After work one evening, I spoke with a friend of mine who was a designer and who, at the time, lived in Johannesburg. He suggested I think about naming my company Tonality. To put it simply, tonality is defined as "the colour scheme or range of tones used in a picture" in the dictionary. And when I thought about it, it perfectly captured what we do in marketing: the tone of everything we communicate is important. The tone of voice My company name holds a special meaning for me, as someone dear to me gifted it to me.

Tonality wasn't merely a label; it defined our goal and strategy. It served as a powerful reminder that the tone we aimed for in all of our content, campaigns, and visual elements had to connect with the audience we were targeting. Furthermore, a dear friend bestowed upon us the personal meaning of our organisation's name. This name had a story behind it that would be meaningful to our clients and partners, as well as to us.

Since your company's name is such a vital part of your brand, you should give it a lot of consideration and use your imagination when selecting it. The previous section about "tonality" illustrates how the process of naming is defined by a combination of theoretical concepts and individual experiences. This demonstrates how essential it is to have a name that is not only marketable but also strategic, in addition to having a great deal of personal significance and connection on a personal level.

When you are searching for a name for your company, it is important to keep in mind that this is your opportunity to give your brand a personality and to set it apart from rival companies on the market. In the same way that "tonality" has been an inspiration for us, let the name of your company serve as a beacon that demonstrates what you believe in, maintains people's interest, and stays relevant over time.

Designing a logo and branding materials

Your company's logo, which serves as a representation of your brand, is where the journey begins. Not only is it a picture, but it is also a powerful symbol that embodies the qualities and values that define your brand.

Your logo should quickly and clearly show what your brand is all about. It should make people feel something and quickly show what your values and mission are. A good logo is easy to remember, even for a short time. Its ease of remembering helps, and its uniqueness sets it apart from others on the market.

Colours, fonts, and images must all work well together to show a clear and consistent brand identity. These parts should fit with the personality of your brand and the message you want to send.

Besides the logo, all of your branding materials, like business cards, letterheads, and online assets, need to use the same design language. This consistency helps people remember your brand and strengthens its identity.

It may be tempting to do it yourself, but professional designers can give your vision a more nuanced and powerful meaning. With their skills, an idea can be turned into a compelling visual identity.

It was a stroke of good fortune that several of my closest friends are also talented graphic designers. The same friend who came up with the idea for the name was also the one who worked on my CI, which stands for "look and feel." Everything I said to him was that this would be an extension of who I am and that I wanted it to be strong and bold. As a result of the fact that he knew me well, he had only one opinion, and I fell head over heels in love with it. It is vital that you, as the owner of a business, have a connection with the brand of your company. When you look at it, it ought to trigger some kind of sense of emotion within you.

Your logo and branding are more than just decorations; they tell the world about your brand's story through pictures. It's important to remember that branding is more than just how something looks. It's about creating a visual language that speaks directly to the heart of your audience and fits with your business's core values.

Using my own experiences as an example, I want you to see this process as a chance to give your brand personality and meaning. Branding should reflect the heart of your business, like it did for me. Make sure that when people see your logo, they connect not only with a product or service but also with a story and a vision.

Creating a Strong Online Presence

The internet is more than just a market in modern business; it is a vast, interconnected ecosystem where people frequently form first impressions online. A strong online presence is not only beneficial to small businesses looking to find their niche, but also necessary. This section of the chapter will take you through the fundamentals of developing a strong online identity for your business.

Consider your website to be the virtual storefront for your business. It is the first place potential customers will discover your brand. It is critical that this online store appear professional, be friendly, and align with the values of your brand. Some important considerations include how easy it is to navigate, how well it works on mobile devices, and how well it matches your brand. A well-designed website attracts visitors and keeps them coming back. It accomplishes this by offering a straightforward user experience that demonstrates how professional your company is.

In this age of connectivity, social media is an excellent platform for brands to interact with one another. Facebook, Instagram, and Twitter are just a few of the many platforms available for connecting with your audience, telling your brand's story, and building a loyal following. By creating engaging content and encouraging genuine conversations, you can transform these platforms into powerful tools for promoting your brand and connecting with your audience.

In the digital world, visibility is crucial, and search engine optimisation (SEO) serves as a means to attain this. You can make it easier for customers to find your company online by improving your website's search engine ranking. SEO entails a strategic approach to writing content, optimising keywords, and developing your site. The goal is to increase your website's visibility and attract targeted visitors.

Content marketing is a strategic approach to creating and sharing useful, regular, and consistent content with the goal of attracting and retaining interested parties. Sharing your knowledge and skills through blogs, videos, or webinars not only benefits your audience but also establishes your brand as an expert in the field. This approach not only attracts new customers, but it also builds trust and belief in you.

In today's digital world, your online reputation can be both your best asset and your worst liability. Customer reviews and feedback have a significant impact on how potential customers perceive a business. Taking charge of your online reputation by responding to feedback and interacting with customers demonstrates that you care about their satisfaction and can significantly improve your brand's reputation.

Using these strategies, you can create a strong online presence that will attract and retain customers, make them loyal to your brand, and help your business grow. Remember that creating a digital presence is an ongoing process that evolves alongside your business and the internet. To create a digital presence that not only reaches but also connects with your target audience, you must be patient, persistent, and adaptable.

Chapter 6: Setting Up Operations

Finding suppliers and vendors

In the business world, your suppliers and vendors are similar to the musicians who perform in a symphony. In order for your attempt to be successful and harmonious, their roles are absolutely necessary. When it comes to running a company, selecting the appropriate business partners is not only a matter of doing business; it is also a strategic choice that will have an impact on the quality, dependability, and efficiency of your operations. The aim of this section is to assist you in selecting and establishing relationships with suppliers and vendors who can contribute to the growth of your small business.

You should begin by conducting research on the various suppliers and vendors operating within your industry. This should be your first step. You should look at businesses that have a solid reputation, a track record of being dependable, and a commitment to providing quality services. It is essential to offer prices that are competitive; however, this should not be done at the expense of the quality of the product or service that you are offering. You can get an idea of how popular they are in the industry by looking at their list of clients, as well as the reviews and testimonials they have received.

One of the best ways to find trustworthy suppliers and vendors is to ask other business owners in your field for recommendations. These endorsements can help you find partners you can trust who have a clear track record. Networking with people in the same line of work can help you figure out which partnerships would be best for your business.

Once you've found possible partners, you should negotiate to come to an agreement that works for everyone. This means talking about prices, payment plans, delivery times, and any other important details. Long-term business relationships are built on agreements that are clear and fair.

Your relationships with your suppliers and vendors are key to making your business work together. Encourage clear communication, honesty, and respect for each other. A strong relationship can lead to better service, special treatment, and useful partnerships that can help your business a lot.

In the beginning, when we were just getting started, I made it my mission to select our suppliers and personally visit their offices to meet with individual representatives.

Although I have not worked directly with them since that time, I still make it a point to check in on them on a regular basis in order to maintain contact with them and to express to them how much I value our relationship.

Through careful selection and ongoing maintenance of relationships with the right suppliers and vendors, you can help your small business become more productive, enhance its quality, and expand its operations. Always keep in mind that these partnerships deserve your undivided attention because they are extremely important to the success of your company and should be given your full attention.

Setting up an office or workspace

When starting a new business, one of the most important steps is to find an appropriate office or workspace. As you progress through this experience, you will encounter challenges and difficulties that will eventually lead you closer to realising your dream of becoming an entrepreneur.

In my own search for the ideal office space, I came across a number of unforeseen events and fortunate coincidences that eventually led to some very useful solutions. Initially, it appeared that everything was going as planned. Following the formation of a partnership, we were able to find the ideal office space that aligned with our objectives and the way we wanted to conduct business. However, life had different plans for me. My partner vanished without a trace, leaving me with no money and an office rental contract approaching its due date.

This challenging time reinforced the value of community and the capacity for adaptation. Not only did my network lead me to a shared office space that not only provided us with the space we required right away but also had a lively atmosphere complete with a coffee shop and idyllic garden, it also helped me get out of a rental contract that was way more than I could afford. Sometimes we have to pass through valleys to get to the peaks.

Whether you're renting office space or setting up a home office, location is a crucial factor. Consider how easy it is for you and your customers to reach the spot. Set aside a specific area of your home if you work from home in order to maintain a more professional mindset.

You must equip your workspace with the necessary tools and technology for your company. A clean and well-organised workspace is associated with increased productivity and flow.

Create an environment that will motivate and inspire you. Improving your mood and productivity in the office is as simple as adding some plants, strategically placed lighting, and a few personal touches.

Establishing your office or workspace bears similarities to the unpredictable and rewarding nature of entrepreneurship. I learned the importance of being adaptable, having a network of people who can assist you, and how much the environment influences how people work. When designing your workspace, remember that it should reflect your vision and help your business grow. Create an environment that nurtures your dreams and fuels your desire to become an entrepreneur.

Hiring employees or outsourcing tasks

Starting your own business is similar to sailing into uncharted waters, where every decision you make will have a significant impact on the course of your journey. There are several important decisions to make, one of which is how you will hire people. The goal of this section is to assist you in making this critical decision by providing examples from my personal experience as well as more general reflections on strategic thinking.

In my experience as an entrepreneur, one of the most important hiring lessons I've learned is that it can be risky for a new company to try to hire a large number of people in a short period of time. The concept of a busy team initially piqued my interest because I believed that having a larger workforce would lead to greater growth and success. However, the reality of overhead expenses and the complexities of teamwork had a significant impact on both me and my company.

When the partnership fell through, leaving me without the funds I had planned, it was clear that we had issues. The team was too large, and the salaries were too high for a startup without funding. A few years later, I realised that a small, dedicated core team that shared the company's values was far more valuable than a larger, less cohesive group. This realisation led me to a model in which I rely on a few key people who are also entrepreneurs and understand the unique challenges of running a small business.

When assembling your team, you should be strategic and weigh the advantages and disadvantages of both hiring and outsourcing tasks.

When you hire dedicated employees, you get people who are deeply committed to your company's goals and success. These individuals are knowledgeable and eager to assist you in your development. However, this requires the small business to handle payroll and benefits and ensure compliance with labour laws, which can be overwhelming.

Outsourcing allows you to draw from a global pool of talent to obtain the specialised skills you need at the time. It saves you money and allows you to concentrate on your main business while professionals handle the details. However, it is critical to be aware of potential issues such as communication breakdowns, quality control, and the confidentiality and security of your company's data.

Whether you hire someone permanently or outsource depends on a number of factors, including your budget, the tasks at hand, and your long-term business objectives. Outsourcing certain tasks, such as accounting or information technology, can help save money on hiring full-time employees. On the other hand, positions that are critical to your company, such as new product development or customer communication, may benefit from having employees who are fully committed to your organisation's culture.

Looking back, I could have avoided some of the early issues if I had balanced my initial excitement and sense of duty for building a large team with a more realistic assessment of my company's needs and resources. The important thing is to strike a balance that is appropriate for your company's goals, culture, and budget. Whether you hire someone, delegate the task, or do both, the goal is to create a team that supports your vision, propels your business forward, and is adaptable to changes that arise as you progress through the stages.

Chapter 7: Launching Your Business

Planning a Successful Launch Event

Looking back, I wish I hadn't missed this turning point in my journey; without it, I would never have had the opportunity to publicly celebrate my company's launch. As a company expands, this event transforms into a significant milestone. This is the moment when you unveil your vision to the public for the first time. This important step was not on the cards for me, which makes me feel like I missed an opportunity to celebrate and spread the word about my business.

A launch event is more than just a party; it is a way to get people excited about your product or service, attract potential customers, and establish your brand in the market. Displaying what you've created allows you to share your enthusiasm and vision with the rest of the world. I didn't pay attention to this step at the time, but now that I know how important it is, I hope to help you celebrate it with the enthusiasm and care it deserves.

Make sure your launch event's objectives are clear and easy to measure. Are you attempting to get people talking about your company, pique the interest of potential investors, or establish connections in your industry? Establishing these objectives early on will help you determine the theme, size, and success metrics for your event, allowing you to easily assess the event's level of success.

Where you hold your event reveals a lot about your brand. It should be consistent with the image of your company, whether that means a sleek and modern space or one that is warm and cosy. The venue's ability to accommodate your expected crowd while remaining true to your brand is critical, as is the convenience it offers your guests.

Planning a launch event is similar to arranging a symphony: every detail must be perfectly coordinated and timed. Your event plan will include a detailed timeline of all tasks, from booking the venue to performing the final sound check. Establishing due dates and responsibilities for each task guarantees its correct and precise completion. Whether an event is well-planned or not, its success hinges on its attendance. Promotion is essential for getting people to come, getting them interested, and ensuring that your launch has an impact beyond the venue. Use social media, the local press, and your network to spread the word about your launch event, making it the talk of the town.

My story does not include a chapter about a major launch, but yours may differ. A well-executed launch event can set the tone for your company and provide the energy and momentum you need to move forward. You are investing in your brand's story and have the opportunity to make a significant impact on the stage of your industry. Take advantage of this opportunity with careful planning and genuine excitement, and use it as a sign that something truly special is about to happen.

Implementing Marketing Strategies

After carefully developing your marketing strategy, the next step is to put it into action. This step is just as important as developing the strategy because it tests your ideas and plans in the real world. In this section, we'll go over the practical steps you can take to bring your marketing strategy to life and ensure it works for your business.

Knowing your target audience inside and out is the most important aspect of marketing. Your marketing efforts must establish a personal connection with your intended demographic for your products or services. Thorough market research is essential because it provides information about your target audience's demographics, preferences, and behaviours. Understanding this enables you to customise your messages and strategies to meet their unique needs and expectations.

Now that you understand who your target market is, it's time to put your marketing strategy into action. This detailed plan should include your marketing objectives, the steps you will take to achieve them, and the strategies you will employ. Using both digital and traditional marketing channels in a balanced way will allow you to reach more people and have a greater impact. Whether it's email marketing, social media campaigns, or print ads, you should use them all to communicate your brand's value proposition to those you want to reach.

The results of your marketing plan will be the true test of how effective it was. Setting key performance indicators (KPIs) and regularly monitoring metrics such as website traffic, engagement rates, and conversion rates can help you determine how effective your strategies are. This data-driven approach enables you to identify what is effective enough for scaling up and what requires strategic improvement or change. Because the market is constantly changing, your marketing strategies must also be flexible. If you're open to new experiences, you might discover new opportunities and insights that can help you improve your marketing efforts. To remain relevant and connected to your target audience, you must experiment with different approaches and be willing to change your plans based on market feedback.

Moving from strategy planning to implementation marks a watershed moment in your company's marketing journey. You can effectively connect with your target market and help your business grow by really knowing your audience, following a well-thought-out plan, carefully checking the results, and remaining open to new information. Keep in mind that the fast-paced business environment necessitates regular reviews and changes to your marketing strategy, which serves as a living blueprint.

Handling customer inquiries and feedback

In the larger context of business, exceptional customer service is more than just a department or a policy; it is a mindset that should guide all aspects of your organisation. It is an important factor in determining your company's longevity and reputation, as well as a reliable predictor of customer loyalty and advocacy.

Throughout my business, my main competitor has made it a point to criticise me whenever possible, but my message to my team has always been to keep our mouths shut and let our work speak for itself. Granted, we lost some clients as a result of what was said, but in retrospect, we realised that they did not share our core values as individuals or as a business.

Customer service is all about exceeding the customer's expectations and ensuring that every interaction they have with your company is positive and memorable. This commitment to customer satisfaction should serve as the foundation for your company's culture, guiding the actions and attitudes of everyone on the team. Remember that satisfied customers are more likely to return and tell their friends about your business. They will be extremely helpful brand ambassadors.

Every business experiences ups and downs along the way. It is not the number of mistakes a company makes that determines its value, but rather how it handles problems. When mistakes occur, how you handle and correct them can have a significant impact on your relationships with customers. Responding to problems in a clear, honest, and timely manner not only helps to resolve immediate issues but also demonstrates your commitment to accountability and continuous improvement.

To provide excellent service, you must first understand your customers' needs, concerns, and feedback. Active listening not only builds trust, but it also shows that you are interested in what they have to say and want to help them in the most effective way possible.

Customers value prompt responses in today's fast-paced world. You show that you value their time and are committed to finding solutions as soon as possible by promptly responding to any questions, concerns, or complaints they may have.

Customising your service to meet the specific needs of each customer demonstrates that you care, which can help your company stand out. Tailored interactions leave a lasting impression, transforming a satisfied customer into a loyal one.

Each employee is essential for providing excellent customer service. You can encourage great service by providing your team with the necessary tools, training, and autonomy to make decisions that are in the best interests of the customer.

It is critical to solicit and respond to customer feedback on a regular basis in order to achieve continuous improvement. Showing that you are listening and committed to improving your service to meet customer needs demonstrates that you care.

In a world full of options, the quality of customer service can sometimes be the deciding factor in determining where loyalties are located. You can lay the groundwork for long-term success by prioritising customer satisfaction, accepting your flaws, and seeing each interaction as an opportunity to impress and satisfy your customers. It is critical to remember that in the business world, the most powerful endorsements come not from your marketing efforts but from satisfied customers who publicly praise you.

Chapter 8: Growing Your Business

Scaling your operations

Starting the process of expanding your business is akin to climbing a steep, unfamiliar mountain. You must be adaptable, plan carefully, and understand how much your business can expand. In retrospect, my own journey through this terrain was characterised by excessive scaling, which highlighted the delicate balance between growth and stability. This personal reflection, combined with strategic insights, is intended to illuminate the path to scaling and help you determine the best time and method for growing your business.

Like many business owners, I was eager to capitalise on the early signs of success and accelerate growth. It appeared that the next step in the growth story would be to choose to grow quickly. However, this significant step, which was not based on a well-thought-out plan, caused unexpected financial strain on the company. The resources were being depleted quickly, and the once-solid foundations began to shake under the weight of the rapid growth. This taught me that scaling is necessary, but it must be done carefully, balancing ambition with operational and financial security.

Using technology to increase efficiency and productivity is an important part of scaling. Automation tools and high-tech software can simplify everything, from customer service to inventory management. This allows your company to handle more work while maintaining high quality and service standards.

Your company's human capital is what keeps it running, and as it grows, you'll need more help than ever before. Employing people who not only have the necessary skills but also share your values and vision is an important part of the hiring process. Even as the business world changes, this will help the team stay motivated and cohesive.

In the ever-changing business landscape, the only constant is change. The ability to adapt to changing market conditions, shifting customer preferences, and technological advancements can all have a significant impact on how well you scale. Maintaining flexibility allows you to adjust your plans in response to real-time feedback and emerging trends. This ensures that your growth is both responsible and environmentally conscious.

Scaling up necessitates a shift in the way your business generates revenue. You must have solid financial planning and monitoring in place to ensure that your expansion does not go beyond the limits of your financial resources. Regular reviews and projections of your financial situation can help you ensure that your growth goals are in line with the realities of your economy. This will keep you from taking on more than you can comfortably handle.

Growing a business presents numerous challenges as well as opportunities. You can approach this critical phase with a balanced perspective if you combine personal lessons with strategic principles. The goal is to grow your business at a sustainable rate that aligns with your primary objectives. This way, growth will benefit your business rather than harm it. When considering scaling, keep in mind that your business will require a different pace and approach than others. To find them, you'll need to combine self-reflection, strategy, and flexibility.

Expanding your product or service offerings

Once your business has established itself in the market, the next step is to look for ways to grow and expand. Adding new products or services to your list is an excellent way to increase growth, attract new customers, and stay ahead of the competition. Let's take a look at the various ways you can broaden your offerings and see how they can help your business grow and succeed.

Adding products or services that complement what you already have in stock is a natural way to begin expanding your business. This strategy not only strengthens your current market position, but it also considers your customers' broader needs and wants. For example, a bakery known for its delicious cakes may begin selling a variety of pastries to cater to a wider range of tastes and events.

You can also expand by discovering new applications for your existing products or services. Adding new versions, variations, or premium versions can provide more options for your customers while also bringing your products up to date. For example, a clothing store could enhance its value proposition by offering custom tailoring services. This would improve the customer experience and generate new revenue.

Your business can expand significantly by entering new markets or focusing on different types of customers. For example, a local service provider may broaden its service area to include neighbouring areas. This could also include demographic expansion, such as a company offering a broader range of products to customers of various ages or lifestyles.

Before you begin growing, you should conduct extensive market research to determine whether your new products will be successful and in demand. Knowing market trends, customer preferences, and how the competition operates can help you plan your diversification strategy, reducing risks and increasing your chances of success.

Just as important is determining how your expansion will impact your finances. You can make informed investment decisions by weighing the costs of developing and releasing new products against the potential revenue. This will help you ensure that your expansion plans are financially viable.

Entrepreneurship is all about trying new things and developing new ideas. Providing a diverse range of products or services demonstrates this spirit, encouraging you to explore uncharted territory and seize new opportunities. Although diversification carries some risks, it is possible to make it work if you plan ahead of time and thoroughly understand your market, as well as your own strengths and weaknesses.

Finally, I want to emphasise that expanding your product or service offerings is an important part of growing your business. It requires you to think strategically, understand your market thoroughly, and be willing to try new things. By carefully following this path, you can guide your business to new opportunities, increased customer value, and consistent growth.

Building long-term relationships with customers

In the complex game of business, the relationship you form with your customers is more than just a connection; it is what keeps your company running. There are many options available, so businesses must be able to not only attract new customers but also retain existing ones. This chapter discusses how to develop long-term relationships with your customers so that they not only buy from you again but also enthusiastically promote your brand.

Excellent customer service is critical to retaining a customer for a long time. It's about exceeding basic expectations, determining what people need before they say it, and dealing with problems quickly and compassionately. A simple transactional interaction evolves into a meaningful relationship when the customer feels heard, valued, and respected. This level of service increases customer loyalty and can convert them into devoted supporters of your company.

Personal touches help your business stand out in a world full of competing demands for your time. Knowing your customers, noticing what they enjoy, and ensuring that your products and services meet their needs demonstrate that your company values them as unique individuals. This personalisation allows you to connect with your customers on a deeper emotional level, increasing the likelihood that they will buy from you again and giving them a sense of belonging.

Building a relationship requires time and does not end with the first sale. Customers will remember your company if you communicate with them frequently through a variety of channels. Staying in touch with customers helps your company become the best option. You can accomplish this by sending out informative newsletters, posting interesting content on social media, or sending personalised emails.

Building long-term relationships with customers is more than a strategy; it is the way you run your business. It's about creating a cycle of trust, loyalty, and mutual value that keeps customers returning and encourages them to spread the word about your company. By prioritising customer satisfaction, personalising experiences, and keeping customers involved, your business can build a loyal customer base that will help it remain successful and grow.

Chapter 9: Overcoming Challenges

Dealing with Failure and Rejection

To be successful in starting your own business, you must not only strive for success but also overcome your fears of rejection and failure. Although terrifying, these experiences are necessary for anyone who wants to become an entrepreneur.

Being in charge of my own business has always stressed me out, and I've always been afraid of rejection whenever I apply for anything. Being responsible for the income of others, especially during times of chaos, which are all too common in environments conducive to the establishment of new businesses, can be overwhelming. The stresses I've been facing have tested my mental strength, pushing me to the edge of my ability to recover.

During these difficult times, the people who have stood by my side and supported me, such as my family, friends, and peers, have been extremely helpful. They have proven to be a strong barrier against the pressures of entrepreneurship. The concept of perseverance, which entails getting up every day to face new challenges, has kept me going, even when things became difficult or I questioned my ability to continue. Although I am still learning how to navigate this journey on a daily basis, my determination to continue has not wavered.

When it comes to business, it's critical to understand that rejection is not a personal attack. On the contrary, you should see it as an opportunity to receive constructive criticism, gain additional knowledge, and improve your approach.

Throughout history, there have been numerous examples of businesspeople who were unsuccessful on multiple occasions before eventually succeeding. Failure should not discourage you from trying; rather, it should teach you valuable lessons and propel you to success.

When things are difficult, having a community of people who care about you can provide you with emotional support as well as practical advice. This network not only allows you to discuss your emotions, but it also gives you new perspectives that can help you overcome difficult situations.

You will face many challenges on your journey to becoming an entrepreneur; however, keeping a positive attitude and looking ahead can help you find your way.

You will become more determined as a result, as well as more aware of new opportunities for advancement.

Entrepreneurship entails more than just achieving external success. Having strong inner fortitude is also essential. On your journey, you will face challenges such as rejection and failure; however, how you respond to these challenges will determine the path you choose. You can navigate the difficult waters of entrepreneurship by learning from your mistakes, relying on your network of support, and staying true to your vision for your company. Remember that success is not the absence of failure but rather the ability to recover from it, learn from it, and try again with renewed vigour and understanding.

Managing stress and burnout

When people talk about entrepreneurs, they usually paint a rosy picture of success and new ideas. However, the bigger picture reveals the more subtle shades of personal struggle and strength. Something that happened to me near the end of the previous year serves as a powerful example of this contradiction. Despite numerous achievements and landmarks, the risk of burnout remained a concern. It manifested as a genuine fear of daily tasks as well as a significant emotional burden. In an unexpected turn of events, a holiday break provided me with a safe place to be and an opportunity to rest and reflect, which ultimately proved to be a watershed moment, re-energising me for the challenges that lay ahead.

This personal story sends a powerful message to all entrepreneurs: self-care and mental health are essential for long-term success.

Because of the nature of the business, it is difficult to distinguish between personal and professional life as an entrepreneur. However, setting boundaries is necessary to maintain equilibrium. To divert your attention away from the tasks at work, it is critical to set aside time for yourself to engage in activities that make you happy. One way to achieve a healthy work-life balance is to give each aspect of your life the attention it requires, rather than giving each aspect equal time.

When you're an entrepreneur, you're responsible for a variety of tasks. Time management is more than simply planning your day. It's also about prioritising tasks based on their importance and impact. It can be easier to stay focused on what's important if you know how to delegate tasks and understand that perfection is frequently the enemy of progress.

Building a business does not have to be a one-person operation. Seeking the support and friendship of other business owners or a mentor can provide both practical and emotional assistance. Talking about problems and experiences with others or a trusted advisor can help you see things differently, feel less alone, and grow stronger.

Self-reflection on a regular basis can help you identify what stresses you out and what triggers you. Mindfulness practices such as meditation and simple breathing exercises can provide you with a much-needed break from the stress of daily life. They can help you centre yourself and face challenges more clearly.

The advantages of rest are numerous. During the holiday season, this became abundantly clear. It is critical to recognise the signs of burnout and give yourself more time to recover from them. And just as wounds take time to heal, the mind needs to rest in order to regain its strength and clarity.

Becoming an entrepreneur entails not only starting a business but also developing one's personality and improving one's overall health. It is possible to handle the challenges of being an entrepreneur with grace and resilience if you recognise the importance of mental health, create a supportive environment, and acknowledge the need for rest and self-care. Keep in mind that the journey is just as important as the destination, and that maintaining your health is an essential component of both.

Adapting to market changes

Entrepreneurs face new challenges and opportunities as the market, consumer preferences, and competitive landscape shift. Simply having a clear vision and a strong desire to succeed in this environment is insufficient. In addition, you must be able to quickly adapt and transform.

One of the first things you should do to maintain your flexibility is to stay on top of market trends. It is critical to monitor industry trends, consumer behaviour, and your competitors' plans. You can anticipate market changes using this ongoing research, allowing your company to respond proactively rather than reactively.

Being adaptable and flexible in business entails being willing to change your plans, experiment with new ideas, and even completely rebuild your business model if necessary. It entails being willing to try new things and open to new concepts. It also entails accepting that not all of your risks will be profitable, but that each attempt is an opportunity to learn something that will help you become a better businessperson.

To adapt effectively, you must be able to listen—that is, hear and respond to what your customers are saying. Their points of view provide valuable information that can help you make business decisions and improve your products so that they better meet market demands.

My own entrepreneurial experience has taught me the importance of adapting to changing circumstances. From a successful start to the arrival of new competitors and shifting market demands, my company's ability to adapt was critical to its survival. We made a strategic shift after realising that our services were becoming less distinctive. We modified our offerings to meet our market's evolving needs. This timely change was not only necessary to ensure our survival, but it also provided us with an opportunity to generate new ideas and position our company for future growth.

Changing with the times in the market should not be a reaction to problems; it should be an intentional part of your business strategy. It requires a culture that prioritises continuous learning, promotes flexibility, and fosters resilience. Making your business flexible from the start ensures that it can survive and thrive even as the market changes.

Being an entrepreneur is like embarking on an adventure through a constantly changing country. Adaptability, based on extensive market knowledge, customer feedback, and a willingness to accept change, is more than a survival skill; it is a strategic requirement for long-term success and new ideas. Our strength as entrepreneurs stems from our ability to deal with change and turn problems into opportunities for new ideas and long-term growth.

Chapter 10: Celebrating Success and Looking to the Future

Reflecting on Your Accomplishments

When attempting to be successful as an entrepreneur, it's easy to become caught up in the day-to-day problems and setbacks, losing sight of the victories and progress you've made. But taking a moment to reflect on your accomplishments is more than just a way to feel good about yourself; it's also an important way to boost confidence, keep things in perspective, and stay motivated for future projects.

Thinking about your past successes is similar to laying the groundwork for your future business ventures. It helps you remember your own strengths and abilities, especially when you're feeling doubtful or troubled. Making a list of your accomplishments, such as academic honours, professional milestones, or personal triumphs, gives you a renewed sense of purpose and confidence.

Identifying the skills and strengths that have helped you succeed in the past can be extremely beneficial when planning for the future of your business. By identifying these characteristics, you can strategically apply them in your new business, ensuring that your unique skills are fully utilised and showcased. This not only helps you explain your value to stakeholders, but it also clarifies your role and approach to entrepreneurship.

When you reflect on your accomplishments, you can set realistic and attainable goals for your business. It helps you determine your potential, which influences both your short-term and long-term goals. This forward-thinking mindset is essential for making future plans and staying motivated during business ups and downs.

A trusted coworker's words sparked a journey of self-reflection that taught me the importance of celebrating every accomplishment, no matter how small. Even though it was difficult to launch a marketing agency during a never-before-seen global crisis, we accomplished incredible things, such as gaining market share without any initial funding and assisting our clients in significantly growing their businesses. This recognition of the past served as a powerful reminder of our group's strength, creativity, and success.

There are numerous obstacles on the path to becoming an entrepreneur, but each one you overcome and each goal you achieve demonstrates how determined and skilled you are. By reviewing your accomplishments on a regular basis, you not only honour your previous efforts but also give yourself the strength to face new challenges with confidence and clarity. Every victory, be it securing funding or witnessing significant growth in your business, represents a significant milestone in your entrepreneurial journey and warrants celebration.

Setting New Goals and Objectives

The process of becoming a business owner is similar to Christopher Columbus' voyage to discover a new world; you have no idea what awaits you before you set sail. Establishing clear goals and objectives is crucial for steering your company towards success, much like a navigator would do to reach their destination. This chapter emphasises the importance of setting clear goals and how those goals can influence your company's growth.

Clear, measurable objectives form the foundation of good goals. Having vague goals like "increase sales" makes it difficult to take action and track progress. Instead, be specific about your goals, such as "increase sales by 20% within the next quarter." This level of detail not only establishes a clear goal but also allows you to track your progress and make data-driven changes.

Even though ambition is what drives entrepreneurs, it's critical to keep your objectives grounded in reality. Setting unrealistic goals can lead to failure and burnout. Consider your resources, the state of the market, and other important factors when establishing goals that are both difficult and achievable. Breaking down large goals into smaller, more manageable steps can help you achieve them and give you a sense of accomplishment and success.

You shouldn't improvise on your business's goals and objectives. They should be consistent with your company's overall vision and mission and assist you in creating the larger picture you desire. This alignment ensures that every goal you set moves your business forward in the right direction, giving your actions meaning and coherence.

Keep in mind that goal-setting is a continuous process that requires periodic reviews and adjustments. The business world is constantly changing, and your objectives may need to shift to accommodate new information and changing circumstances. Review your goals frequently, celebrate small victories along the way, and make any necessary changes to stay on track with your business.

As you begin your business journey, ensure that your goals are clear, attainable, and consistent with your values. These goals will not only keep you and your team focused and motivated, but they will also serve as indicators of success. When you set goals with care, you lay the groundwork for a purposeful and focused business journey. This increases your chances of success and happiness as an entrepreneur.

Creating a Sustainable and Thriving Business

An entrepreneur's dream is to grow his or her business into one that lasts and thrives over time. Your company's ability to remain in business demonstrates its relevance, strength, and responsibility in an ever-changing market. Finally, I'd like to leave you with some thoughts that you should consider whenever you need to make a decision, no matter how big or small.

Your business plan serves as a road map for your company. It includes your goals, market knowledge, and growth and engagement strategies. An effective business plan functions as a road map, providing clarity and direction while also assisting you in obtaining investors, loans, and making decisions.

Customers are the most important aspect of any business. Putting customer satisfaction first entails truly understanding and meeting their needs, providing excellent service, and always adding value. Engaging with your customers, soliciting feedback, and adapting to meet their changing needs can increase loyalty, retain them as customers, and spread positive word-of-mouth about your company.

Innovation is critical for remaining competitive and relevant in a world where technology evolves rapidly and consumer preferences shift frequently. Accept new ideas, technologies, and ways of doing things in order to improve your products and services and run your business more efficiently. When it comes to innovation, being proactive positions your company ahead of the curve, allowing it to lead rather than react.

A successful business has a dynamic team that works collaboratively to achieve its objectives. To foster a culture of innovation, productivity, and mutual support, assemble a team of people with diverse skills who are all committed to the company's goals. Investing in your team's growth and development not only improves their job performance but also increases their engagement and loyalty to the company.

Building a long-term, profitable business is both difficult and rewarding. To be successful, you must understand your market thoroughly, care about your customers and team, and be able to adapt and generate new ideas quickly. Building a solid foundation with a good business plan, a customer-centric approach, an open mind to new ideas, and a helpful team will enable you to achieve long-term success and leave a lasting impression on the business world. Remember that the most successful businesses are those that benefit not only their customers but also their communities and industries. However, most importantly, remember to have fun!

www.ingramcontent.com/pod-product-compliance
Lightning Source LLC
Chambersburg PA
CBHW070956220526
45471CB00007B/3062